The Sacrifice of Continual Praise.

A SERMON

PREACHED IN THE

Reformed Dutch Church,

FLATBUSH, L. I.,

ON THANKSGIVING DAY, NOV. 24, 1864.

BY

REV. CORNELIUS L. WELLS, PASTOR.

[PUBLISHED BY REQUEST OF THE CONSISTORY.]

NEW YORK:
RICHARD BRINKERHOFF,
No. 48 Fulton Street.
1864.

THIS Discourse is printed simply because many of those for whom it was prepared, desired its publication. The Church of God has but one line of duty in this momentous struggle. *Loyalty* is to be her watchword ; *Patriotism* her shining virtue. If I have, in these words of praise, succeeded in quickening the pulses of a single heart, so that its throbs are more in harmony with the music of *Union* and *Nationality*, it is all I ask. Let us, my beloved people, be true to God—be true to man.

C. L. W.

SERMON.

"By Him therefore let us offer the sacrifice of praise to God continually, that is the fruit of our lips, giving thanks to His name."

HEBREWS 13: 15.

I KNOW not how better to begin the attempt to excite in your hearts emotions of gratitude to God, for the mercies of the past year, than by reading the most excellent proclamation of our worthy President, by whose authority we assemble to day:

By the President of the United States of America:

PROCLAMATION.

It has pleased Almighty God to prolong our National life another year, defending us with his guardian care against unfriendly designs from abroad and vouchsafing to us in his mercy many and signal victories over the enemy who is of our own household. It has also pleased our Heavenly Father to favor as well our citizens in their homes, as our soldiers in their camps, and our sailors on the seas, with unusual health. He has largely augmented our free population, by emancipation and by immigration, while he has opened to us new sources of wealth, and has crowned the labor of our working-men, in every department of industry, with abundant reward. Moreover, he has been pleased to animate and inspire our minds and hearts with fortitude, courage, and resolution, sufficient for the great trial of civil war into which we have been brought, by our adherence as a nation to the cause of freedom and humanity, and to afford to us reasonable hopes of an ultimate and happy deliverance from all our dangers and afflictions.

Now therefore I, Abraham Lincoln, President of the United States, do hereby appoint and set apart the last Thursday in November next, as a day which I desire to be observed by all my fellow-citizens, wherever they may then be, as a day of thanksgiving and prayer to Almighty God, the beneficent Creator and Ruler of the universe; and I do further recommend to my fellow-citizens aforesaid, that on that occasion they do reverently humble themselves in the dust, and from thence offer up penitent and fervent prayers and supplications to the Great Disposer of events for a return of the inestimable blessings of peace, union, and harmony throughout the land which it has pleased him to assign as a dwelling-place for ourselves and our posterity throughout all generations.

In testimony whereof I have hereunto set my hand and caused the seal of the United States to be affixed.

Done at the City of Washington, this 20th day of October, in the year of our Lord 1864, and of the Independence of the United States the eighty-ninth.

ABRAHAM LINCOLN.

By the President:

WM. H. SEWARD, Secretary of State.

The spirit of the text and the spirit of this proclamation are the same. The text enjoins the duty of continual praise to God, at all times and under all circumstances; the proclamation utters words of praise, and calls upon the people to acknowledge the Divine hand in the midst of National calamity. In "such a time as this" such words as these are eminently proper. It is true, we do not come to the celebration of our

Annual National Thanksgiving, as it has been our wont, in times past, with banners streaming, with trumpets of jubilee sounding, our hearts exultant, gratitude, joy and praise our only theme. A mighty, overwhelming, irresistible sorrow is upon us. For the fourth time the return of our annual day of praise finds our nation, but yesterday on the high road to prosperity, with a glorious future opening before us, engaged in a terrible civil war. No honest man can for a moment strive to disguise the fact that we have fallen upon evil times. Black clouds have gathered in the clear sky, filled with terrible tempest; they have broken, and now send forth in furious torrents the woe with which they are surcharged. I have no disposition, not even on this day set apart for praise and *thanksgiving*, to cover up, or in any way hide, disaster. To say, peace, peace, when *God* has not spoken peace, is not only useless but absolutely sinful. What then? Setting the disaster before us, in all its dread terror, counting up all the noble heroes who have fallen in battle, marshalling before you all the widows and orphans who mourn comfortless in their bereavement, remembering whole regions of country that teemed with plenty now laid waste, figuring up the enormous debt that day by day steadily piles itself up, as a burden upon our own, and future generations, not forgetting the heavy taxation that so presses, and must long continue to press, upon the industry of the land; taking even that most lugubrious view of national affairs taken and promulgated by quasi traitors and habitual grumblers of every sort, still I ask, *What then*? Shall we forego our annual tribute of thanksgiving to *Almighty God*, the giver of every good and of every perfect gift? As christian patriots we are bound to recognize the hand of God in all events. We do not believe the affairs of nations are outside of His government. On the other hand we know, by even the most superficial study of our Bibles, that in no department of the vast scheme of His providence, is God represented as more directly working than in the rise and fall of nations. "Times of wide-spread and sanguinary disaster are upon our beloved land, but they do not come unsent; the hand of God is in all this conflict. Convulsion, revolution, and war, are but the footsteps of His universal providence in its march through the world." There is therefore no duty more frequently urged in the Bible, than that of continued *thanksgiving*. This is the whole idea of the text; at the same time it is just this disposition that we, as believers in this universal providence, should ever cultivate. The gospel always uses the loving kindness of God, His multiplied mercies, new every morning, repeated every evening, as its crowning argument for repentance. Our own experience has surely often taught us that, in the very heaviest trials we are called upon to endure, we gain our richest consolation from a contemplation of *Divine love*. We are to meet the events of life, not as heathens, but as christians. The old philosophers, groping in the dark, could only see, in the course of events, either a blind chance or inexorable fate. But not thus do we, as christians, come to the discharge of our duty at this hour; but rather by Christ Jesus, the Savior of sinners. "By Him," Jesus, "who sanctifies His people with His own blood," let us offer sacrifice of praise continually. Now, more than ever, since we bow beneath the rod in our

Father's hand, do we need, as we approach the Throne of God, to keep clearly between ourselves and the great Jehovah, *Christ* our advocate. When we see clouds of judgment gather dark and threatening, when the storm pours out its fury, when the very foundations seem unsettled, then it is as at no other time that we feel the presence of our *Mediator*. Christ Jesus and His cause is the central pivot on which all other events turn. Centuries ago, recorded on the pages of prophecy, stands an injunction, to which all the nations of the earth do well to take good heed: "*Be wise now, therefore, oh! ye kings, be instructed, oh! ye judges of the earth. Serve the Lord with fear, and rejoice with trembling. Kiss the Son, lest He be angry, and ye perish from the way, when His wrath is kindled but a little.*" Because I firmly believe in this principle of interpretation, and because in these events of terror, in which we have so deep an interest, I see the hand of God stretched forth to lift up, out of the dust, heaven-born truth, I hail this day of festival and praise with profound gratitude.

If you go forth into a burial-ground you walk over the graves at every step. There is no turmoil here, all is peaceful. The quiet sleepers heed not the sounds of life above them. But this quiet is the quiet of death and festering corruption; to remain thus unbroken until the resurrection trumpet shall awaken the sleepers: then there will be commotion, yawning graves and rising forms, wails of woe and songs of joy. So once there was comparative quiet in our land; peace reigned undisturbed; under her fostering care the arts and sciences flourished, literature advanced, while in every department the nation made rapid progress towards permanent preëminence among the nations of the earth, (thank God that even yet in spite of disaster she holds upon her upward way,) but we were as those who walked over graves and slept above festering corruption; beneath our feet humanity lay buried; justice, and truth, and purity were crushed down into the very bowels of the earth, by the most gigantic political wrong of modern centuries. There was a stirring in the graves—the life-giving resurrection-bearing power of the gospel of Christ Jesus, proclaiming the rights of man to his life, his person, and his liberty, was sent forth over the land; and as, when in spring the south wind blows upon the trees, the buds appear and signs of life are seen, so the nation began to arouse itself under the incitement of this mighty power. The years roll on, years of crime and wrong, until the signs fulfilled, the way prepared, the resurrection trumpet sounded—its blast a blast of woe—then the nation, with a noble heroism unparalleled in history, resolved that, rather than live longer in peace, at the expense of justice and liberty, she would grasp the sword; to do and dare, and if she must, to die, but to perish nobly struggling for the right. We called it night; it was the resurrection morning, though we knew it not. I tell you my friends that we are prone all the time to look only on the surface, at the outside. If God will only give us grace to look down through, to the centre, and see what is really going on, what tremendous and vital principles are involved, what grand conclusions are being reached, what momentous issues are being tried, what glory shines beyond all these clouds; that it is but the irrepressible conflict between right and wrong, truth and error, despotism and liberty, waged the world over and through all time; we shall find to-day reasons for gratitude thick as the leaves of Autumn.

In all the history of our land, as the generations have lived and labored and past away; in all that past so glorious, so secure; a past adorned by the noble names and memories of Washington, and Adams, and Henry, and Jefferson, and Franklin, and Jackson, where will you find, any where, a more fitting season for thanks and adoration to God than you find here, to-day in His sanctuary, under the shadows of His judgments? This is not exaggeration, nor yet the language of unthinking enthusiasm. Let us look at the matter as christian patriots.

I recur again to the proclamation, than which a better, more suitable, less exceptionable, expressive document, has seldom if ever issued from the hand of any executive. I shall follow its order of thought. I cannot help, however, remarking as a preliminary to this, that there is to me something exceedingly gratifying in the fact, that at last custom has established the practice of a "*National Thanksgiving Day.*" The thing itself is old. More than two hundred years ago the pilgrim fathers kept their thanksgiving day on the shores of New England. But hitherto, until this war quickened the pulse of the nation's life, and drew closer the bonds that bind the North together as one people—bonds indissoluble—it was something of only local authority and state institution.

There is cause of praise for any and every course of conduct that in accordance with justice, centralizes and vitalizes our nationality. The seeds of rebellion were planted when it began to be lightly esteemed. If the nation perishes in this contest, let its epitaph be written, *Died of an overdose of State's Rights.* With a territory so vast as that which we possess, with so many diverse elements to be fused together, and moulded into consistency, we cannot exist permanently, unless there be, to some considerable extent at least, a concentration of *Federal* power. We need, and must have, a strong government. If we live at all in the future, it must be as one nation, in all the national territory. Hence it is that I hail with joy every sign of consolidation, because I see, in these, the secret springs of vitality that, in future centuries, shall send forth life-giving blood into every part of the body politic. Keeping these general considerations in view, I pass to the enumeration of some of the many reasons that should lead us to devout thanksgiving:

I. "It has pleased Almighty God to prolong our national life another year; defending us with his guardian care against unfriendly designs from abroad, and vouchsafing to us, in his mercy, many and signal victories over the enemy, who is of our own household."

There is a cause in this for high-sounding praise and loud thanksgiving. Our nationality still lives. Though for four long years the dire disease of civil war has raged fearfully, God has spared us. As a nation we are as yet, in many respects, an experiment. Despotism and absolutism, every where throughout the world, had a sneer ready for a republic such as this, giving to its citizens the widest possible liberty, and conferring the boon of almost universal suffrage. We were gravely told that such a government would do well enough for "the piping times of peace," but could never stand the shock of war, or pass through the ordeal of extensive national disturbance.

And now, since we have stood up, bravely battling with this direful enemy, that has placed his fangs upon our throat, what message of cheer has come from the nations of the earth? With few exceptions, not a word but of scorn and taunting. They have foretold, in their newspapers and in counsels, and their state cabinets, that the wound was incurable, and that the proud, defiant republic of the western continent, must ignobly, terribly fall; standing no longer to rebuke their assumption, or inspire hope in the breasts of the slaves they crushed beneath their thrones. But are they not mistaken? Are we not alive to-day? I do not need to be reminded that this struggle is by no means over, that victory has not as yet crowned our warfare against rebellion, that there is much to be done before we sing the song of final triumph, and that he that putteth on the harness or yet wears it, is not to boast as he that putteth it off. Be it so; at least in this we may rejoice, that God has not as yet delivered us over to their evil prophecies. Those who now contend for this new-born nation may yet, and if God shall give them the victory, will hail the hour of triumph, and witness with exultation the overthrow of the most accursed treason the world has ever seen.

We still live, and our flag floats over a vaster expanse of territory than it did a year ago, floats honored and respected in spite of all the disaster that has come upon us, floats consecrated by the blood of brave men, dearer to-day than ever because it has cost so much. Yes we live, to-day a standing refutation of the kingly lie, so long held and so industriously circulated by the sycophants of the throne, that there could be no strength in a democracy; in a government of the *People.* We live as strong as ever; our sinews hardened; our endurance tested. We live, and grow, and thrive; as grows and thrives some great oak on the rugged hill-side, exposed to storm and whirlwind and tempest; yet striking its roots deeper and deeper into the soil, until, lifting up its head to Heaven, it bids defiance to every gale. Another year of national life. And is this nothing? It is a terrible thing for a nation to die. For them there is no future; for them no resurrection; death is annihilation. Not one of us but that has a fearful stake in the existence and welfare of this Republic. Here all our hopes centre; here our expectations for the future cluster; it is our all. If we thus die, then freedom seems to die, then the problem of man's capacity for self-government is answered in the interest, not of the people and liberty, but of the throne and despotism.

"The citizens of a republic have a special and peculiar interest in its stability and prosperity. Its flags and camps are bound around with the heart-strings of a nation's homes —its hosts move forth to battle with the memories, and sustaining prayers, and heartfelt sympathies of a people's myriad closets and sanctuaries. Linked in with our faith bound up with our trust in Almighty God, our country appeals to every noble sentiment." This is the glory of our republican institutions; around this sacred altar we strike hands together; distinctions forgotten, party differences fading out of sight; while our anthem of humble, yet hearty praise, goes up from thousands of hearts to the throne of the living God. All this is ours, to-day. The memories of the past have just as much power to arouse to enthusiasm as ever, while the noble achievements of the heroes of our own time—our Grant, our Sherman, our Sheridan,—thrill our hearts with joy, we recount their deeds with pride, and hereafter we will delight to tell our children, of the noble men who lived and fought to preserve our dear-bought liberties. Thank God for another year of national life!

But there is in this connection still more that is calculated to lead us to thanksgiving. God has "defended us with His guardian care against unfriendly designs from abroad, and has vouchsafed to us many and signal victories over the foe, who is of our own household." Other nations have been held back from interference in this contest, not from any sympathy with, nor love for, these free institutions; but from the circumstances of the case. They have both respected and feared the nation that was able, upon call, to muster her soldiers, armed and equipped, ready for the fiercest battle, by the hundreds of thousands. This war has developed a power of resistence, and aggression too, if needs be, that has compelled respect throughout all the world. In all this we recognize the hand of God.

Our relations with foreign nations daily grow more and more complicated: so that at times it seems as if collision must be inevitable. From all this we have mercifully been delivered. It is the work of our God, and calls for songs of loudest praise.

The year soon about to close has not been barren of victories gained by our brethren in the field. Some of these achievements are worthy of being written, in golden letters, in the military annals of the world's history. The whole record is filled with deeds of noble daring. Forced marches into an enemy's country, battle after battle fought with an entrenched foe; for days and weeks together sustaining the shock of actual conflict. Who forgets the terrible days of the Wilderness, when the indomitable hero of Vicksburg pertinaciously and bravely fought his way onward; until now, having driven the enemy into the fortifications of his chief city, he waits to crown his work and make the triumph complete? Richmond must and shall fall!

And shall I speak of Sherman, the gallant commander of the Army of the South West? The annals of warfare contain few, if any records so illustrious as the campaign of this army, terminating in the capture of Atlanta; while the noble Farragut unfurls the flag of victory in the harbor of Mobile. For at least one hundred and fifty miles our brave soldiers fought their way over fortified mountains and through swollen streams, guarded at every possible point by bayonet and battery—fighting with a wily, stubborn foe, from day to day, one victory leading to another contest, and thus for nearly three months. From Missionary Ridge to Dalton, from Dalton to Resaca, and Dållas, and Altoon Pass, and Lost Mountain, and on to Marietta; yet on until our victorious hosts enter Atlanta, with banners flying and shouts of victory bursting forth from every heart. And where is Sherman now? Echo answers where? Somewhere in the heart of the enemy's country, piercing the shell of the Confederacy. May God protect him, and crown his bold endeavor with suc cess, is our fervent prayer!

Need I stop to speak of Sheridan; young, bold, intrepid? The victories of the Shenandoah Valley are not eclipsed by any of the whole war. Two rebel generals defeated in succession, and their demoralized army driven in confusion, from one entrenchment to another: whirling through Winchester, pausing at Strasburg, to be again attacked and again defeated. In this campaign the nineteenth of October was a memorable day. Sheridan had fallen back to Cedar Creek. The young commander was absent at Winchester, fifteen miles away. Before daylight an attack is made upon our extended line; the left flank of the eighth corps is turned; twenty pieces of artillery captured; the enemy seem about to regain all that has been wrenched from them by the prowess of our soldiers. But the sounds of battle reach Sheridan, at Winchester, and now he hastens back to the field.

There is something almost sublime in the spectacle presented, of the victorious leader seeking the front of his already retreating troops. The men catch sight of his noble form; new hope inspires them; fresh enthusiasm is born; he flashes the light of his genius, all along that broken line of battle, and turns defeat into victory; and now we are the pursuers; the enemy are routed! Fifty pieces of artillery taken, and many prisoners. The victory was complete.

It would not be easy to estimate the disastrous results that would have been inevitable, if Early had then pierced our lines. The whole valley would have been open to him and we might have been called upon to witness again such scenes as the burning of Chambersburg. Such deliverances are of God and not of man. To Him be all the praise.

I tell you all this was no easy task or slight achievement. It is easy for those who sit in their comfortable homes, secure from harm by the bravery of those who fight *their* battles, to speak slightingly of these accomplishments; when the probability is, that they never have felt interest enough in the contest to make themselves familiar with the geography of the country passed over, or any of the difficulties of the undertaking. Shame on every poltroon, who shall utter a single word of disparagement against our noble citizen soldiers! Let them have our prayers and sympathies, so that, with every blow they strike for God and for humanity, a corresponding throb shall be felt in the nation's heart, while anthems of thanksgiving go up from thousands of christian altars. God bless them, every one. It is well, it is noble, to send them the greetings of loyal hearts, together with provision for their bodily comfort, on this day of thanksgiving; but I will tell you what is better than roast turkey: it is to let them feel in every way, through press, and pulpit, and speech, that they have your confidence, your sympathies, your prayers.

Victories have been gained, and we have the warrant of the word of God, expressed not once or twice, but many times, that, as christians, we have a right to rejoice. "Praise ye the Lord for the avenging of Israel." "O sing unto the Lord a new song, for He hath done marvellous things; His right hand and His holy arm hath gotten Him the victory." And read the eighteenth Psalm, and the twenty-seventh, and the eighty-ninth, and the one hundred and thirty-sixth, and a host of expressions, throughout this precious book, and tell me whether it it is not a christian duty to own the hand of God in National affairs, and to praise Him when He crowns our arms with victory? "We will rejoice in his salvation, and in the name of our God we will set up our banners. Some trust in chariots, and some in horses, but we will remember the name of the Lord our God, "Blessed be the Lord God, our rock, who teacheth our hands to war, and our fingers to fight."

II. "It has also pleased our Heavenly Father to favor, as well our citizens in their homes, as our soldiers in their camps, and our sailors on the seas, with unusual health."

Throughout the North universal health has reigned. No

pestilence has ravaged our land, to add the desolation of its wasting destruction to the fearfully accumulated bereavements that have come upon our households, through the misfortunes of war. We cannot forget either that now, for years in succession, that terrible scourge of the tropics, the yellow-fever, has been withheld, except in limited localities. It has hardly raged anywhere with sufficient violence to be called epidemic.

If here we turn, for a moment, from our contemplation of these themes for public thanksgiving, to our own circumstances, as a community and a Church, we will find that few have greater reason to be grateful than we have. It is true, that some of our loved ones have been taken; some households have been left desolate; hearts have been wrung with sorrow, and tears have flowed from some eyes unused to weep; but these all have been the sorrows ever incident to life, in its best estate; we have dwelt in peace, under the shadow of the divine goodness and mercy. I recall now but two seats, vacant at our sacramental table, that were filled when this year began. But two; and these passed away with a triumphant faith in Him who has for us conquered death and sanctified the tomb. Their going forth, as they passed through the valley of the shadow of death, was noble, sublime. It was no terrible thing for them to die. Both were wives and mothers, fondly loved, tenderly cherished; but they died in peace. They rest in the grave, in hope of a blessed resurrection. We have heard the voice of Jesus say, "I am the resurrection and the life." Blessed hope—glorious triumph over death and the grave!

"Softly within their peaceful resting-place
We lay their wearied limbs, and bid the clay
Press lightly on them till the night be past,
And the far East give note of coming day."

"Short death and darkness! endless life and light!
Short dimming; endless shining in yon sphere
Where all is incorruptible and pure;—
The joy without the pain; the smile without the tear."

They have left us; but our loss is their gain. Still we rejoice, while we thank God for their faith and victory. Thus Christ is gathering home His people; the church militant becomes the church triumphant; while all things are preparing for that glorious hour when "*death shall be swallowed up in victory.*" "*Blessed are the dead which die in the Lord, from henceforth; yea, saith the Spirit, that they may rest from their labors; and their works do follow them.*"

As a community, however, we have been favored with unusual health—a mercy so constant as to be often forgotten, in our enumeration of our reasons for praise; yet a blessing so precious, as we soon learn, when for a time deprived of it, as to call for the most fervent gratitude to the great Giver of every good and perfect gift. But this is not yet all of personal and individual blessing, that should lead us to atune our hearts to praise. We dwell in quiet habitations, and are in the enjoyment of our usual privileges.

It is not so with those parts of our land, where the war

has raged. No noise of strife is heard among us; no destroying army has ravaged our fair fields. The husbandman has sowed, and toiled, and reaped, the abundant harvest, in peace and security. Our sanctuary has been safe from intrusion; from week to week its Sabbath bell has called us to our worship; while the free invitations of the gospel have been given to all alike; and souls have listened, to tremble, to pray and then to believe, rejoicing at last over sins forgiven, a Savior precious, a Heaven secured. Where is there one who, for blessings such as these, will not unite in expressions of thanksgiving? "Bless the Lord, O my soul, and all that is within me, bless His holy name. Bless the Lord, O my soul, and forget not all his benefits. Praise ye the Lord."

III. "He has largely augmented our free population, by emancipation, and by immigration, while he has opened to us new sources of wealth, and has crowned the labor of our working-men, in every department of industry, with abundant reward."

All this in the midst of exhausting civil war. It is a welcome, and propitious fact, that, notwithstanding the ravages of war, the thousands who have fallen, yet there is no perceptible diminution of our population. Strange as it may seem, a country engaged in a contest so gigantic in its character, has yet received accessions to its population sufficient to supply the drain made upon its resources by all the waste incident upon such a state of warfare. From the thickly crowded shores of the old world a living stream has poured itself into this land of the *people.* We welcome them, for our territory is vast and our capacities undeveloped. The broad fertile prairies of the West wait for strong hands, to bring forth from the prolific soil enough to feed, not only our own people, but other nations; nay, develope these resources fully, and a hungry world might come for supply and go away satisfied. If bone and sinew have been wasted, bone and sinew have been supplied; so that, in the face of the demands that have been made upon our voting population, to supply our armies, at the recent election a larger vote was polled in this State at least, than ever before in our history.

Is it asked, with deep concern, is this augmentation of our population, by those who seek this refuge among us, safe? Is there no danger from these turbulent elements? Perhaps there is some danger, though doubtless this peril has been grossly exaggerated; at least, those who have, in times past, raised the loudest cry stand to-day in the closest political fraternization with this foreign element. The danger, fairly estimated, is not greater than may be provided against. Let in upon all classes of society, from the highest to the lowest, the light of the gospel of Jesus Christ; educate, permeate the masses with intelligence, throw open the doors of your school houses, multiply their number indefinitely, and thus you will elevate the people; mould these diverse masses into consistency; while out of it all shall come a nationality founded upon gospel truth, intelligence and virtue.

Our safety lies in the elevation of the common people, of

every nation and of every name, who have cast in their lot with ours. By the ennobling power of knowledge, we may and will, lift what the *slave* aristocracy of the South have termed the mud-sills of society, *up*, so that the whole structure of the body politic shall rise, noble, imposing in its grandeur. The Bible and the common-school are our best defenders. Said one, who had sought refuge in our land from the green isle of the Ocean, that has given more than one noble hero to this war:—

"I landed in America a poor boy; a little trunk contained my earthly possessions; alone and friendless I had my fortune to carve out for myself. I resolved to rise. In America I found, for the first time, helping hands and warm hearts. I knocked at the door of the school-house and it flew open. I went on, step by step; the land of my adoption gave me what I asked,—an *education*,—without money and without price. All that I am I owe to her; all that I am, body, soul and spirit, I lay upon her *altar;* this right hand is pleged to her, and shall ever be raised to strike down the traitor-foe that shall dare assail this heaven-originated *Nationality.*"

He wore the uniform of a major in the volunteer service of the United States. Leaving his studies, preparatory to the gospel ministry, when the sound of war was heard, and the nation's call for volunteers rang through the land, to use his own language, "I buckled on my armor and went marching along." If we are faithful to our own high and solemn duties we have little to fear from the rapid increase of our free population by immigration.

There is, however, yet another source of gain in this direction. Our free population has also been largely augmented by *Emancipation.* The yoke has been broken; chains have fallen from human limbs, and men, made in the divine image accountable, have been ushered from *Slavery* to *Freedom.* Thank God for this! I stand not here, at this late day, to discuss the right or wrong of American slavery. I would not so insult intelligence and piety. Discussion implies doubt. The question has long since passed out of the region of discussion. I should as soon think of constructing a labored argument to prove that adultery, and theft, and murder, were crimes against God. The voice of universal christendom condemns the accursed system. The conscience, the religion of the world, is on record against it. Every denomination of christians in this broad land (I think without exception*) has, through its highest judicature, or Assembly, declared for Liberty and against Slavery. Our own church has, in this way, clearly spoken more than once. Its last utterance, given in June of the current year, was the most decided. The world moves; God is teaching us, by terrible instrumentalities, lessons that should have been intuitions, if we are christians. I read from the five hundred and fourth page of the printed Minutes for 1864,—it is a resolution embodied in the report of the Committee on the state of the Country:—" In times past the General Synod has not deemed it necessary to give forth a judgment, in regard to American slavery, inasmuch as it existed in regions beyond the bounds of our Church;" [yet in

* If there is any exception, it is the Episcopal Church.

1855, when a Classis of the German Reformed Church, in which were professing Christians who were slaveholders, applied for admission into the Reformed Protestant Dutch Church, the Church did speak with practical force, refusing any fellowship with the unclean thing,] "yet as in the overruling providence of that God, who knows how to make the wrath of man to praise Him, there is a prospect opened for the ultimate and entire removal of that system which embodies so much of moral and social evil, and as by such removal, there is opened a wide field of christian labors, to employ the energies of the christian church in this land, the synod expresses its gratitude to God for this bright prospect, and would join in the prayer that the day may be hastened when Liberty shall be effectually and finally proclaimed, throughout all the land, to all the inhabitants thereof." Amen and Amen —God speed the day.

I say, then, that the time for discussion has past. The whole church unites in the prayer that this great evil, that has worked so much of disaster and of ruin, that, in its *damnable* rebellion against a righteous government, has demanded the lives of many of the best and bravest of our young men, be forever obliterated from among us—buried deep, never to rise again. It is a legitimate theme for gratitude to God, that so many hundreds have passed out from under the yoke, to Liberty and self-ownership. Instinctively the soul of every man welcomes *Liberty.* Even the President of the so-called Confederacy, proposes to give it, as a boon to those slaves who shall bravely fight to rivet tighter the chains of their own kindred.

Says Count De Gasparin: "There exists, thank God, between liberty and the gospel, close, eternal, indestructible relations. I know of one species of freedom which contains the germ of all the rest, freedom of soul. Now what was it, if not the gospel, that introduced this freedom into the world? Remember ancient Paganism: neither liberty of conscience, nor liberty of individuals, nor liberty of families—such was its definition. The State laid its hand upon all the inmost part of existence: the creeds of the fathers and the education of the children. Moral slavery also existed every where, and if slavery properly called had been any where wanting, it would have given cause for astonishment. The gospel came, and with it these new phenomena; individual be lief; true independence, makes its advent here on earth; a liberty, worthy of the name, appears finally among men. From this time we see men lifting up their heads; despotism finding its limits; the humblest, the weakest, opposing to it insurmountable barriers."

We will, we must, yet be a free people—the gospel of Jesus Christ; the church of God, shall be the mighty instrumentalities that shall open the prison door to let the oppressed go free. The *night* has been dark, and fearful, and long, but "behold the morning cometh" is the message sent to cheer our hearts, by the watchman from the tower. Yes! the morning cometh, and the day will dawn; the day of

Liberty to all the inhabitants of the land. May God hasten on the hour, in His own good time, in His own good way. O, God, we thank thee for what thou hast already done!

IV. "Moreover God has been pleased to animate and inspire our minds and hearts, with fortitude, courage and resolution, sufficient for the great trial of civil war into which we have been brought, by our adherence, as a nation, to the cause of freedom and humanity, and to afford us reasonable hopes of an ultimate and happy deliverence from all our dangers and afflictions."

True words, fitly spoken, "as apples of gold in pictures of silver." Yes, the great heart of the people beats true to humanity, true to God. Fortitude, courage, and resolution have been inspired; sacrifices have been gladly made, and bravely borne. Who shall measure the costliness of the treasure that this nation has laid upon the altar of liberty. Money has been poured forth without stint; beloved ones have been sent out to brave the perils of the battle-field, followed by the prayers and tears of aching, but God-trusting hearts. The providence of God brought us to the test of virtue; saying to us, I will try your power of physical courage, of sacrifice, of endurance, to see whether,—for the sake of the free and beneficent government bestowed upon you; for the sake of the fathers of the republic, who toiled, and fought, and bled, for the sake of the down-trodden in other lands, who are to-day slowly, but bravely, struggling up toward the light, whom you are to guide,—you will stand up nobly, and quit yourselves like men, to save liberty for America, for the world. Thank God we have stood the test; we have not failed; no not even so much as once. Blessed be God for this; bless Him for the noble daring of our young men, bold to rashness, exemplified by the noble Cushing, blowing up a rebel boat under the very guns of the battery. Bless God for the sturdy courage of the masses of our people, bearing such heavy burdens; for the profuse liberality of our men of business. Most of all bless God for the enthusiastic, hearty patriotism of our women. What were war without the sympathy and gentle ministry of women, terrible enough at best? Rob it of this and it would blacken with tenfold gloom. We bless Him too, with uncovered head, for the noble dead who have given themselves to save and elevate the people. Martyrs to liberty! Their graves shall be ever green; their memories ever fresh in the affections of a grateful people; not one shall be forgotten. Yes, we thank Him for the results of the war. We are a stronger, better people to-day, than we were before the first gun fired at Sumter inaugurated rebellion.

But we should be forgetful of one of the most precious blessings God has bestowed upon us, if we failed to notice the wonderful unanimity with which the people have come up to the mighty task before them, to crush rebellion, once and forever. I have not intended, and do not mean now, to say one word that can be construed into exultation over the issue of the recent election. I have no party shibboleth to lisp; no pet theories to uphold at all hazards; I am but an humble minister of Christ, and it is my duty to flash the light of the gospel, and of truth, upon all questions of duty, upon all the relations of life. I trust I shall ever strive to preach that gospel as a vital, practical thing—not as a dim abstraction—for living men—for men with *hearts*, applied to the real issues of life.

For the manner in which I discharge this duty, I am responsible not to man, nor to consistory or congregation, but to God, I fear not to meet my record, on this score at least, however imperfectly the duty may have been done. I call you, my people, to witness that I have not, for fear of man, failed to declare unto you the whole counsel of God. I submit to every patriot, independent of party, is there not reason for gratitude to God in the unanimity with which the issue was decided? Is it not better so, than with divided counsels,—Congress ruled, it may be, by one party and policy, while the executive seeks to carry out another,—confusion worse confounded? Now you know where to place responsibility: on the broad shoulders of a noble, honest man. To-day, as never before, not even in the memorable spring of sixty-one, we present an unbroken, firm front to the enemy. What is the voice brought to our ears by this result? Is it that all the acts of the administration are endorsed? No, by no means. It says just this, "We, the *people* of the North, say there shall be but one nation in all this territory of the United States." It says, "Here we proclaim to all the world, .hat men are able to govern themselves; that a free republic can and will live, in spite of foreign hate and domestic treason; and that we will defend our rights, thus invaded, to the bitter end—no compromise with armed rebellion, but submission." When rebels lay down their arms, then peace will come; this is the will of the people, not of party, or of faction, but of the people. The great heart of the North beats responsive to this declaration. Here we stand together.

O how miserable little party issues seem, when regarded from the stand-point of "*nationality.*" What are they in comparison with the question, shall this nation live? Nay, can it die? Gathering around the graves of our departed heroes, remembering the glowing example they set before us, of patriotic devotion and self-sacrifice, we clasp hands together, and mutually pledge to our beloved country, our sympathies, our prayers, our lives, our all. To our brethren in the field we say, "Fight on with bravery, firm and true; go forth with alacrity to the battle of the civilized world, where God himself musters the hosts to war." Shall these men who have placed their bodies as a living wall between us and destruction—the destruction of all that we most cherish—shall these men, I ask, ever have to feel that there is behind them a divided country? No, never; God forbid it. Let the sentiment of self-preservation, the first law nature has impressed upon us,—if unmoved by higher motives,—absorb every other feeling. Let every discordant sentiment be melted down in the glowing fire of liberty. In our unity lies our strength. United in a cause so holy, where bound the capacity, or limit the power of these northern states?

Unity must be our battle-cry. Freedom to all men our guiding-star. From this, union will come, and peace will reign; so that some day in the future, (I cannot tell how far distant, for I am no prophet,) there shall go up a loud acclaim of praise to God, for a country purified, regenerated, *free.*

It is because I see signs of unanimity of feeling, daily increasing, that I am ready to rejoice. O! let me but feel that we shall stand together in this glorious work of vindicating free government and the rights of man, then the victory is already won. Light is breaking; hope sits enthroned over the clouds. In the language of the distinguished Frenchman from whom I have already quoted, "Let the friends of America take courage. Who speaks of the end of the United States? This end seemed approaching but lately. In the hour of prosperity, then honor was compromised; esteem for the country was lowered; institutions were becoming corrupted apace; the moment seemed approaching when the confederation, tainted by *slavery,* could not but perish with it. Now everything has a changed aspect; take confidence then, lovers of freedom, for its greatness is now inseparable, thank God, from the cause of justice. *Justice cannot do wrong.* I like to recall this maxim when I consider the present state of America."

Who shall speak of dissolution? We shall not die, but live! If liberty, driven from other lands, is suffered to expire here, from whence is it ever to emerge? It is for us to decide, whether freedom shall yet survive, or be covered with a funeral pall, wrapped in eternal gloom; this is the tremendous issue we are trying to-day. Let it stand forth distinct and clear. No wonder despots sneer, or that lordly aristocracies that have grown great, and rich, and strong, upon the labors of the people, sympathize with our slavery-nurtured foes. No wonder the down-trodden of all lands; the wronged and the crushed; the little ones of earth whom Christ owns as His peculiar care, *pray* for our triumph. Their prayers will be heard and answered.

I cannot close with words more fitting, than in the language of the eloquent Robert Hall, addressed to the soldiers of England, about to go forth to meet the armies of the first Napoleon; and it it is a prayer most suitable to ascend to heaven on such a day as this, in behalf of our own cherished army and its beloved commander. "And Thou, sole ruler among the children of men, to whom the shields of the earth belong, gird on thy sword, thou most mighty, go forth with our hosts in the day of battle; impart, in addition to hereditary courage, that confidence of success that springs from thy presence; pour into their hearts the spirit of departed heroes, and inspire them with thine own; and while led by thy hand and fighting under thy banners, open thou their eyes to behold, in every valley, and in every plain, that which the prophet beheld by the same illumination: *chariots* of fire, and *horses* of fire; '*then shall the strong man be as tow, and the maker of it as a spark, and they shall both burn together, and none shall quench them.'* " If God be for us who can be against us? We go back not one step.

* * * "One voice, like the sound in the cloud,
When the roar of the storm waxes loud and more loud,
Wherever the foot of the freeman hath pressed,
From the Delaware's marge to the lake of the west;
On the South going breezes shall deepen and glow
'Till the land it sweeps over shall tremble, below
The voice of a people up-risen, awake,
America's watch-word, with freedom at stake,
Thrilling up from each valley, flung down from each height,
Our country and liberty! God for the right! "

www.ingramcontent.com/pod-product-compliance
Lightning Source LLC
LaVergne TN
LVHW021200120826
845150LV00011B/2337

* 9 7 8 1 4 1 8 1 9 3 9 9 7 *